Y'ol

Birhan Keskin

TRANSLATED FROM THE TURKISH BY
MURAT NEMET-NEJAT

Spuyten Duyvil
New York City

Translation © 2018 Murat Nemet-Nejat
ISBN 978-1-947980-61-7
Cover photo: Muhsin Akgün
Library of Congress Cataloging-in-Publication Data

Names: Keskin, Birhan, 1963- author. | Nemet-Nejat, Murat, translator.
Title: Y'ol / by Birhan Keskin ; translated by Murat Nemet-Nejat.
Description: New York City : Spuyten Duyvil, [2018]
Identifiers: LCCN 2018023104 | ISBN 9781947980617
Classification: LCC PL248.K456 A2 2018 | DDC 894/.3514--dc23
LC record available at https://lccn.loc.gov/2018023104

at the bifurcation they part
Y

"The loveliest part... the road teaches how to walk my friend, the one who never grows stale."

GÜLTEN AKIN

casting pebbles

Offering
(or a bit of accounting)

Every day once I tried to return to this book. Every day once I walked out of the house and walked with a broken cloud. Every day looked at someone and bent my head. Every day I looked at a newspaper with vacant eyes. Every day someone talked, I pretended to listen. Every day once I asked myself where am I, every day once a northern winter settled in me. Every day I looked at your photographs before me. Every day I got angry once and once I asked myself why did I get attached so much? Every day I thought of justice and cruelty. May be of everything. Every day I walked in the street with a barbarian and the civilized. I opened every day the minarets with the sounds of the morning azan. Every day I tried to part a curtain. Every day I thought I understood nothing, every day thought I understood it all. I saw pigeons off. Every day I thought I could not stand the day. I stacked books one under the other and magazines rolled next to each other. Things that were a blur walked along with me. Every "totality" I saw stuck in me like a knife, couldn't understand it. Every day I pulled a piece of stone out of me. Every day I implored sleep to take me in its arms. Every day, day is ending but not the night, I said to myself. Every day I saw things didn't console me. I asked myself why we remember the days of separation afterwards as a fog. Don't forget your anger, I said to myself, if you forget, you fall. I reserved at least one hour every day to standing up erect. Every day I ran through my heart the word "lifelong" at least once. Every day the word "lifelong" pinged like coal in my heart. Every day once I called you silently "my love." Every day once I called you "heartless." Every day I thought of two old women sitting side by side and looking at each other with tenderness. Every day I said that photograph of these women is torn. Every day once I said "ah" and once I took it back. Every day I said "my road companion" and I covered my face with sorrow. Every day I tasted your bitterness. Every day not to forget but not not to forget I applied poison to my heart. Every day I thought to become human how many faults she is hiding in herself. Every day I tried to open a lock. There was something else, there was something else: I had called out to you with the voice of the earth, and not the voice of the world. What is an ordeal or what is a sin? What do they matter to me anyway. You were the center of the world everyday, and I the endless land maaaaaarks receding from you.

III

Because you regarded as too much my weeping after you
take these rocks they're yours... and from now on
let all the drums pound, the oud strings snap
scream to the void, together.
We'll cough up blood
blood
blood
Since the world is so cruel,
Unbecoming our heart.

Let all the drums echo,
what comes from the void
strike what fills the void
echoes   in the void

See how the one sleeping on ashes is coughing up
blood blood
blood
let them know

IV

I... and every time
Whatever life could teach the ash
it has taught me.

(...)
I must have slept a long time in the ash
I slept a long time in the ash
I slept a long time in the ash.

II

The scream obstructed inside is lamenting outside
towards morning
sleep is refusing me
from outside somewhere a loooong
waiiiiil is erupting.
inside me the walls of cruelty.
sleeeeep take meeeee
in your arms.

when i get up
trudging along to the bathroom looking
sounds are breaking loose from my eyes.
inside then these tears flowing silently are yours are
saying. in the walls inside me
these stones are welled,
pulling out a sound i can't pull out,
walled in the silence *silence* of the stones,
thick, primal, towards the void, from the antechamber of the night
tttwaaaards mooourningg:

I let you loooose on this lying world at last,
bitterly, bitteeeracidly

VI

me, you always, my love,
me, you always
i read it from the words flowing from your face
i cast a spell of love on your eyes, i cast a spell of compassion on your hands
your mother disowned you
i wove you
into my life.

V

Don't expect me to burn
I have burnt a lot, you know it.
I can't burn, can't
can't my ashes are flying.
the gilette blade you plied in my dreams is in my flesh.
without bleeding without hurting.
without
hurting
this world is ice, ice
ssssssss nothing's
hurting

is false,
false what i'm saying
false, what you're saying
becoming only
this world.

I'm already ash
ash ash aaah ash
if anything left
inside the ash my humanity's
rising.

Let the world see now.
whiiiiite seeing
off on iiiiice
me
(liiice on iiice
white)
coughing up
blood

I

as they stood apart
the other calls the one who isn't here:
they're next to each other, when under each other
the world widens.
one offers the other fire
and like those with a different meaning
from an old book carrying their becoming with themselves
in an ooold book, then to add warmth
they're adding a fairy tale
but yet becoming another fairy tale
transcending their becoming.
the other calls the one who isn't there
that's how magic becomes magic.
the other calls the one who isn't there:
were they fairy tales...
Taiiiils...

VII

the world's nothing
compared to the dome i built for you
let it collapse, let it go
—stars are imploding under—
as easy to doubt, as to believe
loose yourself to the world, or stay with me
i loved you so much beyond the world that
that we call it offering our heads as sacrifice on your roaaad
us the barbarians.

VIII

broken down, yes, i broke down that edifice of lies:

fur LLLIes to reveaLLL themselves striPPed nakeDDD

you're my nest
i your   S

IX

Casting me to a world i don't know

condemned, with no sentence of my own, sileeeeeeenced.

our dream was called aging together, that's why, maybe,
it hurts so. do you expect sentences of love from me
without the unity which is a sentence?
doooon't.
two women preparing jam in the kitchen. with red peppers, etc.
a windy hill. looking out on both sides,
horiiizon, etc.,
as if the earth not a circle but slightly an ellipse.
besides, two women not quite up to the curvatures of the earth, etc.
that's how it was. I'd believed her, as i believed myself.
to talk about love that's beyond what's love! aaaah!
It was a dogma... just.
that's why i am so diffused,
shoveled into this world.
what do you want me to say?
i have a tooth irritated by the air.
that's why my silence, my speech.
besides i was offended when i didn't die by the initial pain.
first became human then.
or or i was remodeled from what was left.
which i remembered surrendering to the pain
one doesn't die, i remembered,
one doesn't diiii
iiie

ah, from the depth of asia....

XI

Be fair, even when suffering, told me.
be fair! aren't you the one who believes that life is a throw of dice
even directing fortune one should
be part of Fortune, etc.
therefore, why, you be fair now!
shut up. don't say such things! be
fair!

You don't believe them, do you?
cast me into a world i don't know, aiiii
say

I say,
everything remains as words, aaaare words,
i say,
you call that just?

X

Oh, the one who doesn't hear the person
oh, the big mistake they call life,
...

Oh, the one i wouldn't trade for anyone
why is your departure so heavy?

where is Justice?
from one november to the other
one side of me blind, the other deaf.

XIII

All apart, i'm all apaaaaar-
t and all is here: Aprin Çor Tigin
Haşim, Kadı Burhanettin
all here. blind, lame and loon-
y screaaaaaming:
Let it cool a little,
cooool down, down coool.
let your bits and pieces cool a little
when rejoined
you'll be something else.

XV

I don't waaaant to be something else
didn't want something else.

with patience, my love, with patience,
saying
saying
let our hurts be equalized.
patience of the sort where it passes from the flesh
reaching the heart. only, with patience

in this city.
how many people in this city
in this city converted their soul
intooo a dooooome for you!

XIV

it implied a great sorrow, i saw and understood,
the love of the one passing from the flesh to the heart.
next to it my darling next to it
the flesh's betrayal,
in short,
is a little thing.

XII

let this be an elf in a tall tale
in a short story
let the elf take my weary head
take my words my sentence my hooole
leave them (oh, i left them gently, see) in your heart.

I am in no state
to serve this sentence no mooooore

XXXI

Suffering is wounds rubbing against each other
building its nest in love, between disappearance
and being, and the thing gnawing at the wood
is the wood,
inside,
a person searching for a nest is idling in vain but
is pursuing the nest part of the pursuit.

The outside, darling, the outside, what is it
but a conglomeration of roads making you a fugitive.
roads that keep leaving, horizontal
roads, ah,
that's why i was hung up on the idea of a dome:
a dome which is a kind of 180 degree object,
oh
possible, possible with a great desire.
Woven into the known and forgotten senses of strife.

XVI

As sand
as sand
blow

deeeescend
you are saying
to me
from the scruff
of time

you, whisperer of justice
my cruel one, be
just there,
think: of the house
which was the holiest seclusion
an upward
drift,
who struck whom in **her** deepest seclusion?

XVIII

To taste, my love,
the bitterest

you wanted
me

to taste, sweet.

XVII

you took the keel of your sail boat
took the sail boat of your spine
took the spine of your keel

why?

XIX

Between being and non-being
am i,
i am so always
anyhow
not knowing
why
how i'm stitched together

between being and non-being
between being and non-being
a broken pitcher in my hand

a broken pitcher in my hand
where shall i leave it.

XX

Is being lost to depart or to remain I'm at a loss to tell
any more
like furniture feeling uncomfortable in its place always
but believing, oh believing, that leaving changes nothing

and not knowing, .. maybe that's why
i'm like a solemn oath delivered from a wrong spot
maybe i wanted i wanted to return to the house
that wounds me at the same place always.

XXI

Ah, if I say it with my voice
no one would believe me
because it resembles no other language

But the sky i return, return return
return to is you toooo
yuuuu

you are the glad light
that strikes my dark life
makes my water wave

XXXV

Loved her at the supreme level of your being.
don't tremble any more my heart.

forgive yourself and her,
let her go.
go.

your fate from the day of its inscription
you'll be loving her a thousand times more... a thousand times more
anyhow.

XXII

So that days elapse by themselves
I stood behind a window
So that none
touches me
no medicine be balm to my hurt
if the cure will occur, let it be
by itself
that I stood behind the window
staring at life flowing and saw time collapsing.

I know, have known, too well I know,
when it passes, it has passed,
when you waned, when my ache has waned
and I have mended, then I will face
the bland taste of emergence from pain

everything biiiiiiiiiiiiiitter.

XXXIII

What do you think,
what did you think?
What is miiiine
is also your fortune;

Mountain slash
the wounded solitude

there

XXIII

We won't get better, Ilhan's saying
We won't, know that.
I knew that: it was heavy
Knew: very heavy
Knew: every step of the way
...

With you, my love
I am unluckyly happy

XXIV

Does a fairy tale have the heft of a stone,
it seems it would.
Together wanted wanted to believe in a fairy tale
you and I,

that simple.

you left me step
by step
        by step
left me.

am i
now in a state to carry
a stone,
to lift
a stone,

to cast
a stone...

XXV

Mine is a sad life, yes,
a sad sodden earth,
not with reality, not with truth,
built with my heart's
blind
mind
a sad
sodden
life.

Not alone, I know,
not alone,
there are a thousand others, a ten thousand others,
that pass by
on the sodden
earth.

you will live
now onward
patched up with reality's patch work.
but I darling, I darling,
am still carousing with

the spirits

SUUUUDDENLY.

XXVII

Cheetah before my eyes, Gooooo
ooooooooooof

The fool inside me is climbing Mount Fuji to yo.....
don't rain on my eyes with an old letter
the world's entire set of neons on and off
and a snap shot torn apart with two blades.

I am covered with sores like a hippopotamus,
do you understand that?
Inside my giraffe looking afar
at telephone poles

soon I will die, where is the water I must drink?

XXX

Snow with a fierce wind and a broken heart reached the midnight hour of your white mountain. D I S P A R A T E let me cry for what i have lost you... for what you have

XXVIII

I had promised my life.
you took it and broke it into bits.
why don't you mention the name of justice here also?
juuuuust iz...
that's why my great wound
my great anger

do not
eeeeeeend
all iiiiinside
reeeeevenge
fuuul

full of replies'

re-plenitude

XXVI.

Such a long road, arrived with you.
now bifurcated
you apart

i, a part

Y why

must we
travel this road
together?

when we were so...
on our side plains, trees, trembling
winds flew. did we know then
of our joint
road
road accidents, road tiredness,
roadness
itself?

              Ro   de
                a

XXXII

next to you I was like someone whose life is passing in exile
didn't you hear it, I said it many times,
in that long exile,
how intoning *justice justice* you reduced yourself to
flour grains,
seeing and hearing,
seeing and hearing, the world sequestering
from you

You didn't know that, in order not to go berserk in your exile
I lived in a starred dome woven by the mind
of my soul

In the middle of **consoulation** lies the soul,
its finality, my darling,
didn't you see it?

in the middle of *Justice*
lies the tyrant?

XXIX

Later, very much later, at the end of these pieces
remember me
as a mom who loves her daughter
a lot

me, who was never able to rejoin yo-
uuuuu

XXXXII

And at peace inside there was a soft light
outside a redness surrounding the mountains
To remain outside the World, this was a good reason
and a key instrument
striking the keys of the piano with an exquisite music.
In your face a gratefulness that I felt having seen the world.
a winter burying and putting to sleep the harshness of everything
Imagine, say it snowed at the Grand Teutons.
In the middle of that snow before us a river
mixed with snow,
flowing.

Don't turn me pale and yellow   pale, and yellow,
don't.

XXXXIII

You are too human, my darling, too human,
whereas I'm a barbarian, a beast
my tongue talks of forgiveness, for giving it
for free and yours of justice
revenge

Is there a need to say it, my love
to say it now
the ace sniper I raised shO OOO t me
the snows of Klimanjaro my love
snows of Klimanjaro
sl iiiiii ding down

XXXIV

If you love someone, don't kill her, saying it
is easy whereas each love is first to herself
then the other an executioner.
and in love death has a meaning, "an act in style
must have its disruption," let us say
every fire first grazes its side

so from now on every time you see the shadow of a poet
darkened by the smoke left after a fire,
aimless, restless, passive, static, still
still smoldering
or a sister weeping to her partridge,
far away, with the sound of clarinet on her breast wandering

XXXVI

After such a long time why I didn't touch her
why I didn't pull out my weapons
tucking everything that happened into my heart and withdrew
you ask me...
if i have not touched her,

not touched her
is only for one reason...

barbarians lay hands only on equally barbarians.

XXXVII

I resemble grass lying aslant in the flowing street
branches pulling left and right by the wind.
because of love wounding with betrayal is it love?
oh, the nook of my liver, burning burning
my heartstrings breaking, tie me.

XXXXI

If I had left one breath of life I'd breathe it on you
They will say: the dungeon in her was too high
should've have seen, touched, caressed, without teaching
without telling her to put wings and arms to her fate, I
having lost her, I burn now, I burn particularly
for that.
I could not fix the places I broke
I could not fix the places I broke

I had clung to you with a last breath.
That was the worst, the worst.

XXXIX

Love, between two people is what is never =
I am not a Divan poet darling
to chisel lines for you
nevertheless, on the spur of the moment,
I'd like people to know my attraction for your eyes, your hands, your feet.
I'm of this mad times, this venomous moments
the poet, in smithereens. What can I say,
still, in me, from very ooold times,
Ah, Lei... Ah, Leilaaaaa
I left your name on a cold desert night.

XXXVIII

There are two cherries on a branch
between love and anger
burning *a*burning, parted *a*part.
Let this love stop. Love, take five!
Oh, the wild one!
Insurrection
InsurrectiOOOn!

Tie the space between my legs.

XXXX

My love, as if she's staying
All words, as if they're staying
Because love, love because
it wants a path, an ideology for itself.

I know, some ages are tumbleweed in the desert wind,
you my love, ahead, a bit ahead in time
you will start your history, that place
starts with my history.

And count, backwards, one by one
let them stay with you now, take them
these stones.

the old world

Parting the Branches

The roaring of the forest will end, when?
I'm full of scratches for a thousand years, parting the branches.
In that place... where trees become visible one by one... is it far?
A sylvan bombardment. We'd spent long, a very long winter,
and a summer stretch... lie down a little, a little. Not so scary as
we worried, at least with kids in the summer.
And it was a secluded rare rose of the world, the spring.
Did we skip it without smelling it, smelling it?
What occasionally reveals itself is the g-spot of routine without
ever parting the branches, without ever. But with no smelling?
I saw. She, feeling dizzy because of the shaking of trees
the world was feeling dizzy. Spare for me in the monotony of the prairie,
the routine of the meadows, the placidity of the river, only this occasional
revealing. Once more.
Only those times. Spare them for me. Once more.

A slightly high plateau, before mountains show their majesty.

Horses

They were like the wind, with them we were also like the wind.
Their absence now
an empty space.
That must be the reason why
the sound of the grass is so far away now.
...

They were like the wind, with them we were also like the wind.
Passing the clouds, the grass, the meadows we touched the river.
Migrating to the mountains, descending the mountains we lived by our names.
Life is a lightning strike we said, we learned it from them.
Our youth was the burning sun, the proud wind.
Our aged carried rain on their faces, grew their hair... aaaah,
wee said... d... d... d.

Horses that suffer my grief, flattening the hills.
Horses that warm my heart.
A brown evening is round here, horses aren't.

My Taiga

Two exiles, their tongue stolen in them and on the road.

The whole night sitting down we scribbled on blank papers.
That must be a way of being silent a long time.
I am a swatch of cloth, caught on a tree.
For a while you drew women with slanting eyes in the sand.

This isn't our house, and this place
can not be our home, this is not our house, not our place,
we kept repeating, and, keeping repeating,
we were on the road so many years.

But we're already at some familar place,
a weeping, whose tears have dried and
a windy slope inside us.

Keep This Letter

Here, a long time, in *this* station I stayed.
I was *there*, now.
This place is the station *beyond* limbo. I had written to you of my state
of limbo once..
You'd cried when you'd read that tale of purgotory
and I when I wrote it. *Stop!*.. I'd cried a lot.
I'd cried like like Niobe[1]:
*"You should not have let me cry, you should not have made me stare at the road.
Those professions of love, those professions of love don't forget."*

This is the stop *after* the limbo. I'd waited a long time there.
Here I will stay! *Stay*!

I realize now the earth is spherical. It turns. *Make it stop.*
I've nothing to do with those that turn, I will say. *Stop.*
I used to turn in my time also... I turned. Then stopped..
I have no energy to turn. Stop.

LET M EE STOP AND S T OP

I N OW AM A RU I NE D S T   A T I ON

I AM R ET AIN E D IN MY H E A R T DET A I N ED

---

1 The specific reference in the original is to Esrâr Dede who was an 18th century mystic Sufi poet. Weeping, suffering is an integral part of Turkish Sufism. Ecstatic suffering, expressed in tears, replaces the ecstasy induced by wine in Rumi's poetry.

A Blind Depth

Beyond my ability to write to see to hear my inner life
has escaped into yours. With a fine, fine, long, long thread.

reaching the distance of your waters of your road of its sleep...

reaching my inside: the blind depth the blind layers the blind cluster

a frog is standing, *there*! Blind..
not hearing me, a frog's standing *there*, not seeing me..

covered at the top, blue, dust at the top: a memory

..

doesn't wake up, gas, doesn't wake up, dust.

I tried to wa k e
                       it
up.
It
doesn't knoow,
me.

Cool In the Shade

Meandering across the whole spectrum of the scene, the sun
hits
(hits the trees of the plain one by one,
hits the phosphorescent skirt of the water, hits the farthest point of the river).
I have a pain that the sun can't hit the bottom of
is my pain so secret, so deep
that my tongue couldn't call up,
it didn't come up.
It's waiting atop a tongueless rock
has been freezing a long time there, has been freezing
most.

To Become Two

Those, the grass,
                    are not here. I told you.
So much time has passed, I waited too long. You don't have to
they're not still here.
I'm staying, waiting, they're not here.
I waited too long.. Just like this
I hardened myself. *staaayed*. Became a stone. They're not here.
Later someone broke my stone.
Tipped over towards you. I became two. They're not here.

The road was advancing before me, and inside mountains leaning sideways.
Someone open'd me up, *SAW*. The silver image of time
and sharp crystal
                    pouring tears.

The Swan's Complaint

The total is this: the grass on the wayside..

My face always faces the water. It keeps getting lost in it..
This lake; the world in which I spent a
                               lifetime.
This my staying
                 put here, so that the dream keeps growing... *growing*
These nestlings, spreading our wings
our breasts grazing each other, etc....
As wide as this lake you see. And plus the grass on the water's edge...

If you're swan, if you're sworn into this life of love
I'll tell you: if you leave... and become a knot somewhere else.

But there were those who left and I saw what happened to them.
(In everyone who left there was a *sparseness*, a someth'ng... and you flew but
what you *saw there*?)
I chose not to, *stayed* over and *o'er*, the snarl.

What I learnt: If a swan is sworn into love as into her life
The whole world's a lake, the curvature of the neck doesn't end.

İLHAN İLHAN

I. We're talking about the sadness passing through me.

II. The dome has dimensions, they should also have names, you're saying.

III You know also that amazement is a silver moment passing through the body.

IV. I who always looked at the sky, always looked at the sky.

V. There are two things that, that you never forget, you're saying.

VI. "Finally, finally have you decided on a beloved?"

VII. You'd stayed, you are staying. I heard your were staying.

Ankara 2

I can not add any more to this scorched letter
to describe my state
I put a few blades of grass bent by the wind
among its pages
You, understand the rest.

Ankara,
I am your partridge, a black ring round my neck.

The Red Chief

Love also is patient,
the orange dawn is ready, *wait*.
Tether your horse in the shade of the poplar.
Where love overflows
look at the grass, the leaves, *wait*.
It'll be even harder ahead if you don't,
wait,

let it go, let the ear hear some of the sounds,
let the heart hear them,
wait.

The Prairie of Final Union

You tagged and burnt me so! you knew what burning was.
Now that you know, what? Tell me

Did your word ever ache,
you are vile, did your word ever ache like this?
I gave my soul
                to my word. it rose,
I hurt the height, just like that!
I suffered anything that came. I forgot my blood, just like that!

You're a property of earth, just like *this*!
I made it to the morning, something achin' inside me.

You burnt me, I thought you're burning for me just like that.

Just watch how the burning goes. see, I made myself ash.
You, *stay* in this low ground. I left for grass.

Human Being

...

I outgrew my actions in joy
and arrived at the place
where one stands with grief
with the long and silent thread of a fury I crouched
under the pure light of day.

...

Defeated... but forgotten, sad
I'm not,
believe me
because their passion for the world was large.
From my heart
that was covered under the voices of grass
I extracted my horse that was attached to the shade of the poplar.
The road's once again mine.

...

The human being is a sentence
wandering between the apex of the sky and the basement floor
and always right
wanting to come to a place where one can say I arrived
hidden in that object called life.

"I am not proud of being different, I'm completely opposed to separations, Judge!"

AHMET GÜNTAN

The Other

But you'll rise all white
while they'll remain black below!
Let your head stay in the clouds, they're foot soldiers in mud!
Attend to your sweet dreams, while they'll sweat and pump!
You bring down the knife to the melon's skin, they'll run.
You grow fat in the center, let'em be squeezed in the corner!

They are those staring at a distance in a flimsy discarded photo.
Those who carry water to a stone all their lives.
They are those standing frozen in a memory.
They are those, burnt, sleeping in the ashes.

You have violet eyes, they're all green-eyed monsters!
Ah, how you're immortal on this earth, they merely dead.
And you smell so nice, a human paradigm
They corner dirt, they trash, they shit.

And you are bells and whistles, the others masses.
What will these ignorami, these san-culottes, these barbarians do with light? they're a total loss.

As you were saying "*It was very amazing, it was so much fun*"[2]
They were begging forgiveness from a tree's spirit.

Your balcony is too high... so giddying.
But the world will soon be very low... it seems.

Birhan Keskin

translated by Murat Nemet-Nejat

---

2 "*It was very amazing, it was so much fun*" is uttered in English in the original Turkish text.

Birhan Keskin's Y'ol[3]
Murat Nemet-Nejat

Birhan Keskin's (1963-) Y'ol is about a love affair between two women that through breakup, loss and suffering becomes transformed into a spiritual, potentially divine experience. In that respect, it follows the path of the quintessential story of Turkish poetry, *Leila and Majnun*, where Majnun loses his beloved Leila whose family refuses to give her to him. He goes insane ("Majnun" means crazy, lost, a vagabond). When finally her family relents and bring her to him, he does not recognize her (he says, "you are not Leila"), so transformed was his love for her to a spiritual state of becoming. The very title of the poem points to this metamorphosis. "Yol" means "road" in Turkish, which Keskin deconstructs by adding an apostrophe after "Y." The last two letters "ol" means "become." In other words, the title says "the road of/ towards becoming."

In the essay "A Godless Sufism: Ideas on the Twentieth-Century Turkish Poetry"[4] I argue that, though the word "god" is almost never mentioned, a spirituality which I call "godless Sufism" permeates modern Turkish poetry. The essay caused quite a controversy in literary circles at its first publication in 1995 and was attacked by all sides. The secularists thought I was infiltrating religion back into the language of poetry after Atatürk's reforms. The religious people thought I was being blasphemous. In effect, I was doing neither. I was just pointing to something that to me was "hidden in plain sight": Turkish character is deeply, inescapably spiritual—often tinged with a violent eroticism— and its poetry reflects it. A yearning spirituality, full of tears and suffering, is at the core of its power. Because 20th century Turkish after Atatürk's linguistic reforms had discarded a lot of the Arabic and Persian vocabulary that embodied the spiritual/erotic Sufism of those two languages (particularly of Persian and Hafiz's poetry), modern Turkish poets had to pursue and rediscover it in the agglutinations of the Turkish syntax and its pantheistic connections to a pre-Islamic central Asian landscape. In this interaction between spirituality and syntax (which I call Eda) Turkish poetry gains its stunning originality. Shifting the focus of attention from vocabulary to the intonations, cadences of

---

3 Metis Yayinlari (Istanbul: Turkey), 2006
4 *Eda: An Anthology of Contemporary Turkish Poetry* (Talisman House, Jersey City, 2004), pp. 323/34.

an infinitely flexible and suggestive syntax, Turkish poetry became an ideal, potent vehicle for suppressed communication—be it sexual, political or religious.

Birhan Keskin's poetry, particularly *Yol*, is in the middle of this tradition, Eda. In fact, the first written response to "godless Sufism" occurred in a review of Birhan Keskin's poetry by the Turkish poet Ahmet Güntan in *Kitap-lik*. Güntan said that he was at first bothered by the word "godless" because it seemed to belie his own belief in God. Then, he realized that the term "godless Sufism" referred to a presence, not spelled out; but pervasive in Keskin's and many other Turkish poets' work without their being quite aware of it. The term brought to consciousness, revealed the spiritual core of their writing: that "god" was perhaps the most suppressed word, the invisible pervasive presence, hidden in plain sight in secularist Turkey.

Yol consists of two parts: "taş parçaları" and "eski dünya." "taş parçaları" consists of forty-four "fragments" ("parçaları") which are sinuous, austere coloratura[5] songs focusing on the two lovers, their intimate moments, their quarrels, their alienation from each other. "eski dünya" consists of thirteen pieces. Their tones are more leisurely, philosophical. They are poems of ironic, often heart-wrenching arrivals. A Central Asian landscape of prairies, mountains, plains—the area where originally Turks came from—permeates them.

The present manuscript consists of the entirety of the book, all the poems appearing in the same order as in the Turkish original.

Murat Nemet-Nejat

---

[5] Keskin stretches certain vowels or consonants in "taş parçaları" in the style of Turkish classical singers like Safiye Aylar.

A Few Notes On Translating Birhan Keskin's Y'ol.

During a long interview that covered many subjects in Turkish for a Turkish journal, here is the way I described my processes translating Birhan Keskin's Y'ol[6]: "... The 'sound of the poem,' in the traditional sense, does not represent the totality of the poem. For instance, the 'sound' in the poetry of Eda is silent. Its music is among the words, in the movement the sentence creates as it develops, in its cadence. The 'sound' of Eda is a sinuous, linear movement of thought, as it evolves full of emotion and longing."

Birhan Keskin's Y'ol is exactly such a line. It is something that is simultaneously seen and heard. I began the translation of Y'ol with the fragments in "casting pebbles." In many of these pieces in Turkish there are spots like "yoooooğğğğğğğ" ("...") or "uffffffffffffuk" ("...") that are reminiscent of concrete poems. These are spots that suddenly stop the poem from being read aloud, "voiced out," creating cracks, silences—voices that can be uttered freely in the mountains, but in the daily world of suffering and hurt are suppressed, silenced. The second section of Y'ol "the old world" starts in the mountains, the woods. The language of this part is opener, more relaxed, a language that uses longer lines [though the suffering is never far below the surface/water level].

Translating Y'ol, I had on my mind the American blues, the voice of Billy Holliday and the Turkish singer Safiye Aylar's singing style. In American English, the blues lyrics constitute a treasure chest of tangential, elliptical language. Everything in blues is expressed in coded fragments. Particularly in the last years of her life, Billy Holliday's voice is full of "imperfections." The unforgettable beauty of her voice lies in the variations in tempo and harmony she creates with her words. In other words, in Holliday's language, while singing, there is something reminiscent of the fluid word order of the Turkish syntax and Eda's cadences. While reading words like "yoooooğğğğğğğ" in Y'ol that reminded me of concrete poems, I thought of the way Safiye Aylar stretches with diamond-like clarity the vowels in her songs. An emotional, almost operatic force is hidden in the spare language of "casting pebbles." Translating "casting pebbles," my problem was to synthesize those "visual impurities," obstacles, with the rest of the language of the fragments to point to the emotional power hidden in them that flared out through these obstacles.

---

6 The translation from the original interview is my own:

I want to thank the Cunda Translation Workshop at Cunda, Turkey, and its organizers Saliha Paker and Mel Kenne, and its sponsors T.R. Ministry of Culture and Tourism and Boğaziçi University, where, in 2011, my intitial steps in translating the entirety of Yol began.

I want to thank Metis, the publishers of *Yol*, for granting the permission to publish the English translation of Yol by Spuyten Duyvil in the United States.

BIRHAN KESKIN was born in Kırklareli, a town on the European side of Turkey, in 1963. She graduated from the literature department of Istanbul University in sociology in 1986. She published her first poem in 1984. Between 1995 and 98, with her friends, she published the literary journal *Göçebe* (*Nomad*). She worked as an editor in numerous publications.

Her poetry books are: *Delilirikler* (*Madlyrics*), İskenderiye Library Publications, 1991; *Bakarsın Üzgün Dönerim* (*You Will Find That I Will Return* Sad), Era Publishers, 1994; *Cinayet Kışı* (*The Winter of Murders*) + *İki Mektup* (*Two Letters*), Göçebe Poetry Books, 1996; *Yirmi Lak Tablet* (*Twenty Milligram Pills*) + *Yolcunun Siyah Bavulu* (*The Traveler's Black Suitcase*), YKY, 1999; *Yeryüzü Halleri* (*The World's Conditions*), YKY, 2002; *Kim Bağışlayacak Beni* (her first five books, *Who Will Spare Me*), Metis Publishers, 2005; *Ba* (*Ba*), Metis Publishers, 2005; *Yol* (*Yol*), Metis Publishers, 2006); *Soğuk Kazı* (*The Cold Excavation*), Metis Publishers, 2010); *Fakir Kene* (*The Poor Tick*), Metis Publishers, 2016).

Birhan Keskin's *Ba* won the Altın Portakal (Golden Orange) poetry prize in Turkey in 2006. Her Soğuk Kazi won the Metin Altıok poetry prize in 2016.

MURAT NEMET-NEJAT's recent work includes the poems *Animals of Dawn* (Talisman, 2016), Th*e Spiritual Life of Replicants* (Talisman, 2011), the collaboration with the poet Standard Schaefer "Alphabet Dialogues/Penis Monologues"; the translations Seyhan Erözçelik's *Rosestrikes and Coffee Grinds* (Talisman, 2010), the republication by Green Integer Press of Ece Ayhan's *A Blind Cat Black and Orthodoxies* (2015); and the essays "Dear Charles, Letters from a Turk: Mayan Letters, Herman Melville and *Eda*" (*Letters for Olson,* edited by Benjamin Hollander, Spuyten Duyvil, 2016), "Holiness and Jewish Rebellion: 'Questions of Accent' Twenty Years Afterward" (*Languages of Modern Jewish Cultures: Comparative Perspectives, edited by Joshua L. Miller and Anita Norich* (University of Michigan Press, 2016) and "İstanbul Noir" (*Istanbul: Metamorphoses In an Imperial City,* edited by M. Akif Kirecci and Edward Foster (Talisman, 2011). He is the editor of *Eda: An Anthology of Contemporary Turkish Poetry* (Talisman, 2004).

Murat Nemet-Nejat is presently working on the poems *Camels and Weasels* and *Io's Song*, and a collection of translations from the Turkish poet Sami Baydar. *Camels & Weasels* is part of a seven-part serial poem *The Structure of Escape* which also includes the poems *The Spiritual Life of Replicants* and *Animals of Dawn*.

www.ingramcontent.com/pod-product-compliance
Lightning Source LLC
Chambersburg PA
CBHW030102100526
44591CB00008B/241